CORPSE FLOWER

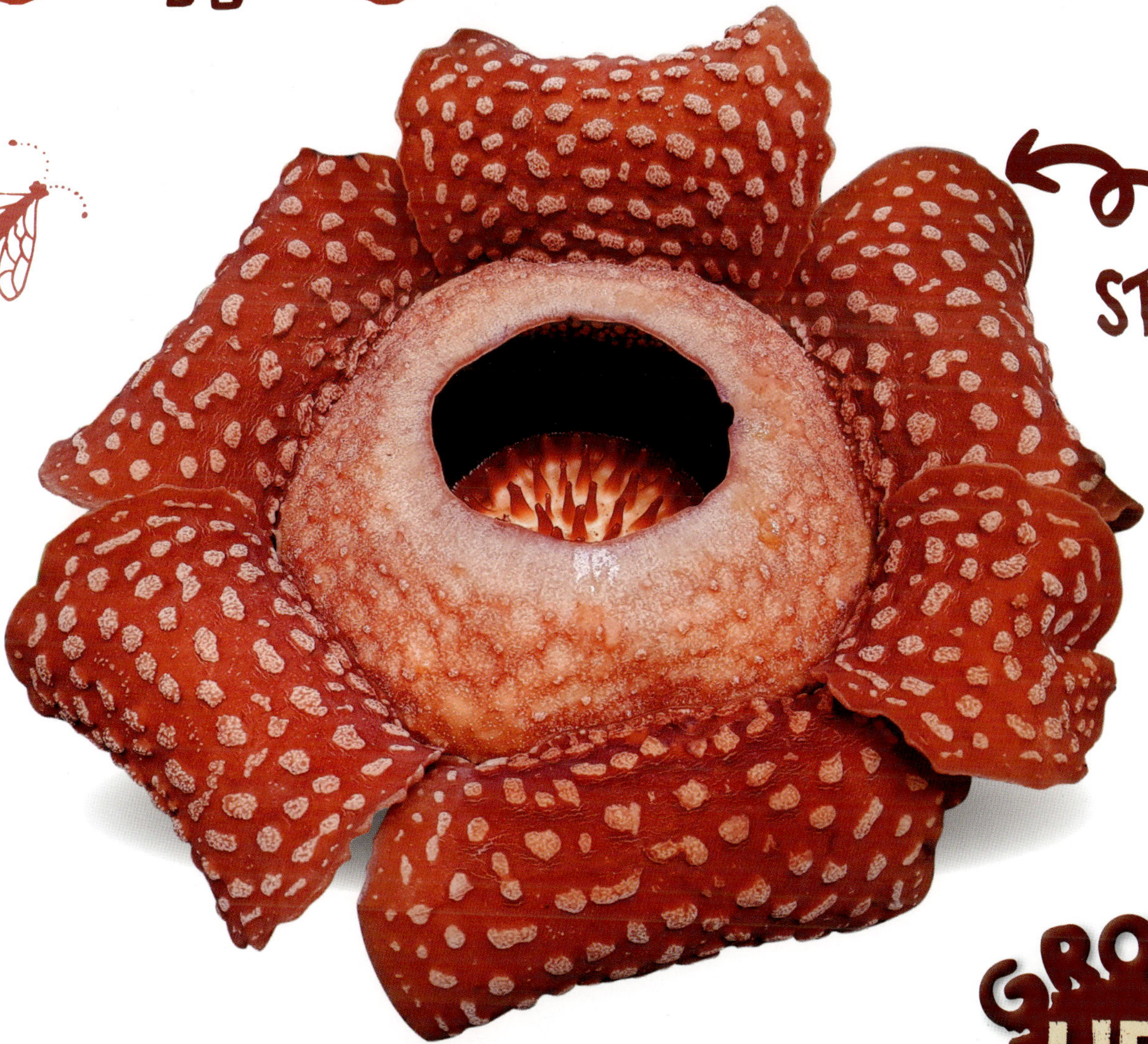

STINKY!

by William Anthony

Please visit our website, www.enslow.com. For a free color catalog of all our high-quality books, call toll free 1-800-398-2504 or fax 1-877-980-4454.

Cataloging-in-Publication Data

Names: Anthony, William.
Title: Corpse flower / William Anthony.
Description: New York : Enslow Publishing, 2022. | Series: Gross life cycles | Includes glossary and index.
Identifiers: ISBN 9781978526433 (pbk.) | ISBN 9781978526457 (library bound) | ISBN 9781978526440 (6 pack) | ISBN 9781978526464 (ebook)
Subjects: LCSH: Amorphophallus–Juvenile literature.
Classification: LCC QK495.A685 A68 2022 | DDC 584'.64–dc23

© 2022 Booklife Publishing
This edition is published by arrangement with Booklife Publishing

Published in 2022 by
Enslow Publishing
29 E. 21st Street
New York, NY 10010

Written by: William Anthony
Edited by: Emilie Dufresne
Designer: Amy Li

All rights reserved. No part of this book may be reproduced in any form without permission in writing from the publisher, except by a reviewer.

Printed in the United States of America

CPSIA compliance information: Batch #CWENS22: For further information contact Enslow Publishing, New York, New York, at 1-800-398-2504.

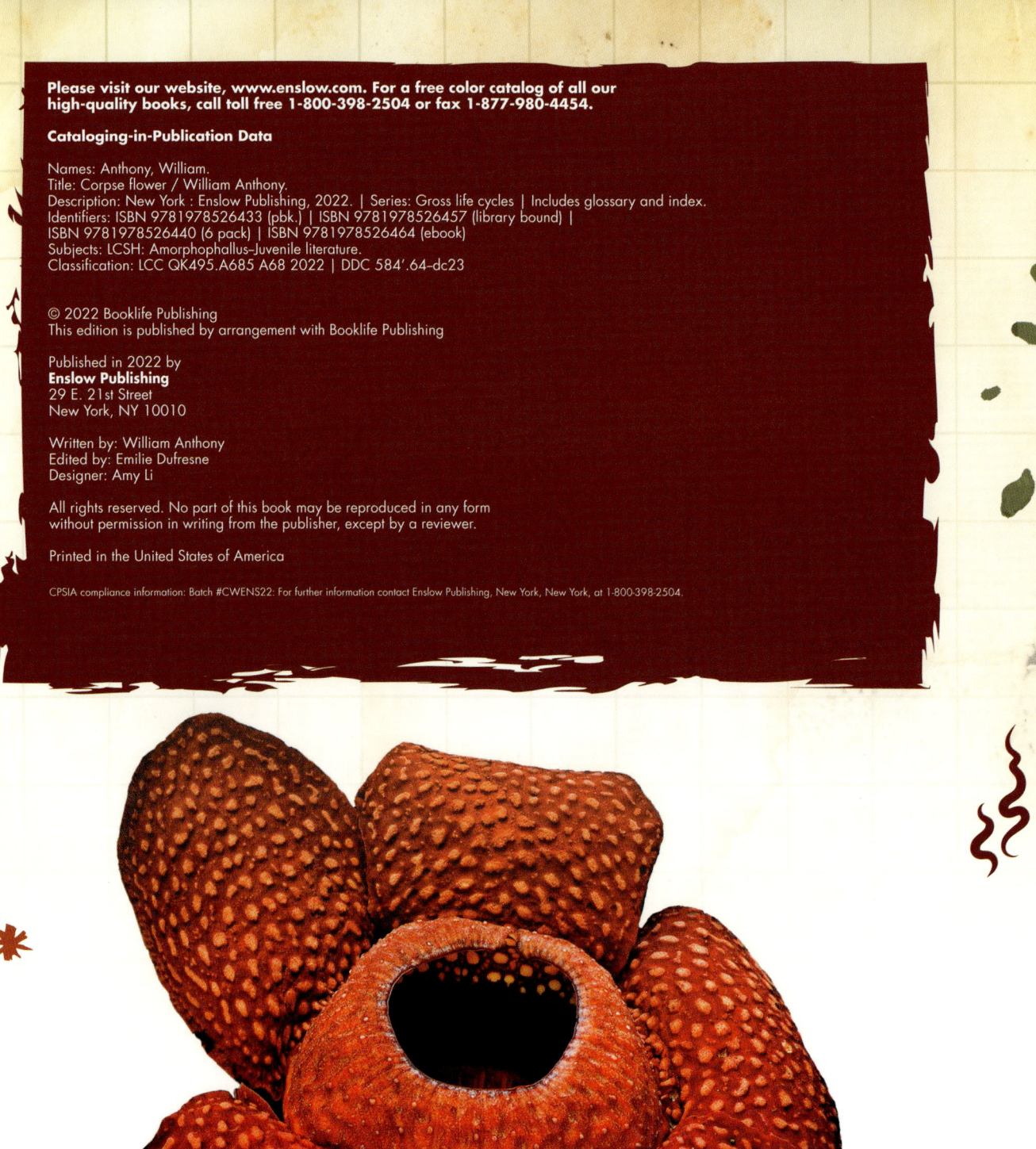

CORPSE FLOWER

Page 4	What Is a Life Cycle?
Page 5	Gross Life Cycles
Page 6	What Is a Corpse Flower?
Page 8	It Starts with Poop
Page 10	Best Buds
Page 12	Parasite Plant
Page 14	Stinky, Stinky
Page 16	Fruity Treats
Page 18	A Gross Life
Page 22	Gross Life Cycle of a Corpse Flower
Page 23	Get Exploring!
Page 24	Glossary and Index

Words that look like **this** can be found in the glossary on page 24.

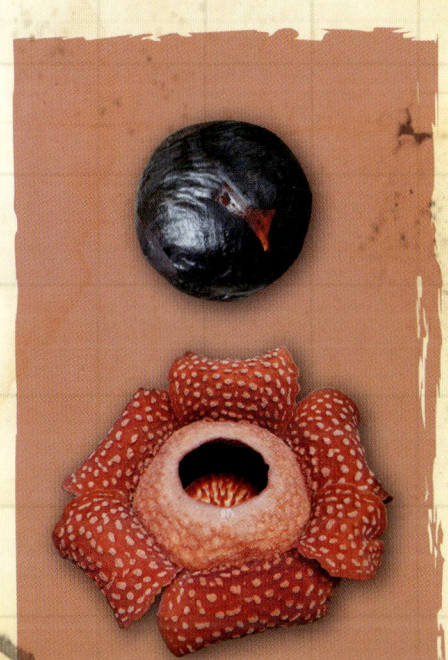

WHAT IS A LIFE CYCLE?

All animals, plants, and humans go through different stages of life as they grow and change. This is called a life cycle.

human life cycle

 baby →  child → adult

GROSS LIFE CYCLES

Not all life cycles are the same. They can be quick or slow. They can have lots of steps or very few. And some can be absolutely GROSS!

Life cycles can be oozy, gooey, and full of nasty smells. Gross!

WHAT IS A CORPSE FLOWER?

A corpse flower is a type of large plant. It can be found in the **forests** of a few countries in southeast Asia, such as Indonesia and Malaysia.

Corpse flowers have a disgusting, gross life cycle. There's a lot of stinky smells, creepy-crawlies, and yucky poop. Are you sure you still want to read on?

IT STARTS WITH POOP

Who do you think could help the plant?

The corpse flower grows fruits. To **reproduce**, it needs to spread the **seeds** from these fruits all over the forest. Because the plant cannot move itself, it needs help.

The plant is helped by animals such as the tree shrew. Animals eat the corpse flower's fruits. The seeds from the fruit come out in the animals' poop, spreading them around the forest.

tree shrew

BEST BUDS

Many plants have the same main parts. They have **roots**, a stem, leaves, and flowers. They use these parts to get water and **nutrients**, as well as to make their own food.

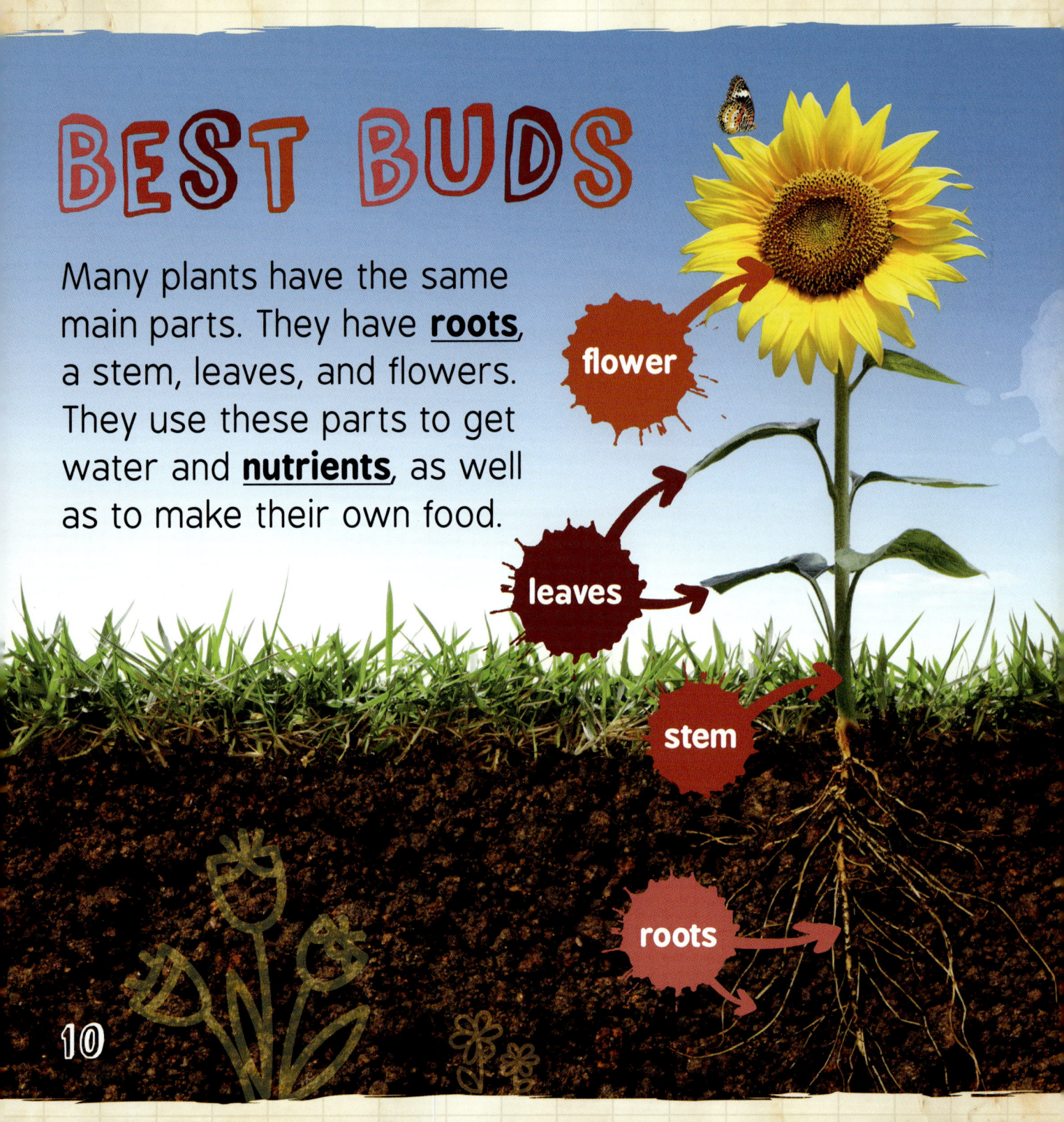

corpse flower bud

If a corpse flower seed falls on the correct type of plant, a bud will grow. However, corpse flower buds do not have roots, a stem, or leaves like other plants.

PARASITE PLANT

Stealing food and water helps the bud grow into a flower like this one.

The corpse flower cannot get water or make food for itself because it has no roots or leaves. Instead, it digs into the vine it grows on and steals its food and water!

Parasites are living things that live on or in another living thing, which is called the host, and take food from it. Here, the corpse flower is the parasite and the vine is the host.

STiNKY, STiNKY

The corpse flower needs to be **pollinated** to make more fruits and seeds. **Insects** help the flower do this.

The corpse flower **attracts** insects in the grossest way.

14

Can you spot the fly inside this corpse flower?

The corpse flower smells like **rotting**, dead animals. Yuck! Insects love the smell and pollinate corpse flowers as they travel between them.

FRUITY TREATS

It's the end for this parasite.

Once an insect has pollinated the corpse flower, it can make its fruits. The corpse flower only **blooms** for around one week. After that, it dies.

As one corpse flower dies, another may begin its life cycle. The fruit gets eaten by animals that poop the seeds out, and everything starts again.

A GROSS LIFE

The corpse flower doesn't just have a gross life cycle. It's pretty gross altogether! Did you know that one type of corpse flower could be used to make injuries heal faster?

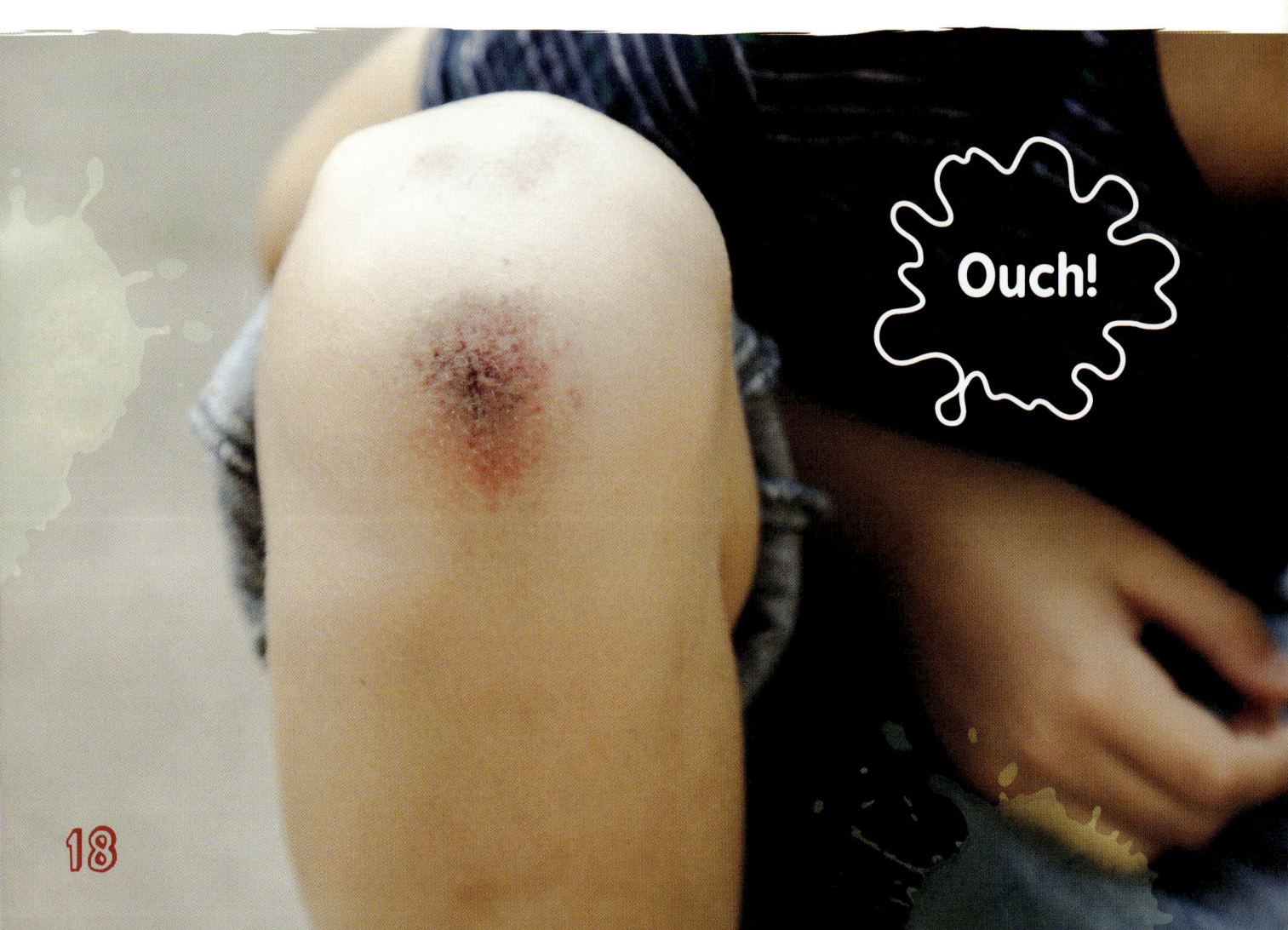

Ouch!

The titan arum is also known as the corpse flower.

There is more than one flower known as a corpse flower. They are commonly said to smell like sweaty socks, dead fish, onions, or garlic. Ew!

The corpse flower holds a world record for being the largest flower in the world. It can grow to around 3 feet (1 m) wide. That's about the same as a four-year-old child lying down!

When the corpse flower dies after around one week, it turns into a gross, black, slimy mess.

21

GROSS LIFE CYCLE OF A CORPSE FLOWER

1 Animals eat the corpse flower fruit and spread the seeds in their poop.

2 A bud grows and steals food from its host.

3 The flower attracts insects with its gross smell.

4 Insects pollinate the plant, which then makes fruits.

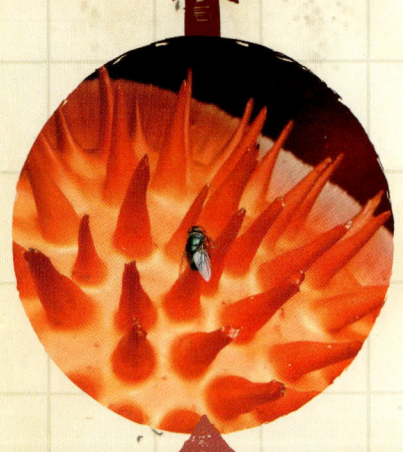

GROSS LIFE CYCLES

Get Exploring!

It can be difficult to see corpse flowers in nature because of where they live. But there are many flower shows you could visit to learn about flowers!

These flowers smell much nicer than the corpse flower!

GLOSSARY

attracts — Causes someone or something to move toward a place.
blooms — Makes a flower.
bud — A small part that grows on a plant that will grow into a flower, leaf, or new branch.
forests — Lots of trees and bushes that cover large areas.
insects — Animals with one or two pairs of wings, six legs, and no backbone.
nutrients — Things that plants, animals, and people need to live and grow.
pollinated — Given pollen from another plant of the same kind so that seeds will be made.
reproduce — To make more of the same thing.
roots — The parts of a plant that grow underground, take in water, and hold it in place.
rotting — Slowly breaking down.
seeds — Small objects made by a plant from which new plants can grow.

INDEX

buds 11–12, 22
food 10, 12–13, 22
fruit 8–9, 14, 16–17, 22
hosts 13, 22
insects 14–16, 22
leaves 10–12
parasites 13, 16
pollination 14–16
poop 7, 9, 17, 22
roots 10–12
seeds 8–9, 11, 14, 17, 22
smell 5, 7, 15, 19, 22
stems 10–11
vines 12–13
water 10, 12

PHOTO CREDITS

Images are courtesy of Shutterstock.com. With thanks to Getty Images, Thinkstock Photo, and iStockphoto.

Recurring images – Milan M (grunge shapes), Sonechko57 (splat shapes), Jojje, Infinity32829 (paper background), Rimma Z (watercolour splatters), Sopelkin, olnik_y, nikiteev_konstantin (decorative vectors). Cover and p1–2 – Doctor Letters, zulazhar, Rebellion Works, p2–3 – Norman Ong, zulazhar, Mohd KhairilX, p4–5 – Pixel-Shot, Gelpi, Samuel Borges Photography, 3445128471, p6–7 – Anna ART, David S Wills, p8–9 – skajornyot wildlife photograph, Aelita17, p10–11 – Christian Edelmann, ifong, p12–13 – dherrmann79, Darren Kurnia, p14–15 – Samoli, Siti Farhana Ahamad Azhar, p16–17 – Luca Brianza, Ilya Andriyanov, p18–19 – Andrii Oleksiienko, Isabelle Ohara, p20–21 – Alex M9, Herrieynaha, p22–23 – Siti Farhana Ahamad, Azhar, Prettyawesome, Mazur Travel, kajornyot wildlife photography, Christian Edelmann